Who Ai and Serena Williams?

by James Buckley Jr.

illustrated by Andrew Thomson

Penguin Workshop

To all young athletes who dream of golden glory:
Nothing comes without hard work!—JB

For Rhia—AT

PENGUIN WORKSHOP
An Imprint of Penguin Random House LLC, New York

Visit us online at www.penguinrandomhouse.com.

Library of Congress Control Number: 2017021534

ISBN 9780515158038   19 18 17 16 15 14 13

Contents

Who Are Venus and Serena Williams?

At the 1999 Lipton Championships tennis tournament in Florida, eighteen-year-old Venus Williams stared across the net at her opponent. It was the final match. Venus had won this same tournament a year earlier. She was moving up the world rankings and was among the top young players in the world. Her opponent was pretty good, too. She had won sixteen straight matches, the most in the world at that time, and she was also Venus's younger sister, Serena. Off the court, they were family. On the court, they were rivals.

This was a historic match. It was the first time that sisters had faced off in a major professional tennis tournament final since 1884! Tennis fans around the world were thrilled to watch these two young stars battle. (Earlier in the year, the two sisters had each won a tournament on the same day—a first in world tennis!)

At the Lipton Championships in Florida, both players wanted to win, but both also knew they would feel bad for whichever sister lost.

"Why would I want that to come between someone who has always been around, always been a very special friend for me? I couldn't imagine that and I don't think she could either," Serena said.

The sisters knew they would still love each other no matter what. But . . . someone had to win and someone had to lose.

A player who wins six games wins a set, and Venus, a year older and more experienced, won the first set, six games to one. Women's tennis matches are best-out-of-three sets. Serena roared back to win the second set, six games to four. Tied at one set apiece, whoever won the third and deciding set would be the champion. In that third set, the sisters were tied at four games apiece when Serena made several errors. That gave Venus an opening. She won two straight games, giving her the set and the match.

That championship match in Florida was the first of what would become thirty-one sister vs. sister matches over the course of their careers. When they were not playing each other, Serena and Venus Williams beat just about everyone else they played.

Together, the Williams sisters have transformed tennis. Both have been ranked No. 1 in the world and both have rooms full of trophies and championship medals. Their powerful styles of play have changed women's tennis forever. Their fashion sense and drive to win have made them heroes and role models to millions. Their African American heritage also stands out in a sport that has traditionally been nearly all white.

It hasn't always been easy. They have battled injuries and illness, faced tragedy, and dealt with racism. Along the way, there were some people who didn't want them to succeed.

But Venus and Serena just kept playing. They were determined not to let anything stop them from winning. Not even each other.

CHAPTER 1
Cracked Courts

Richard Williams was a divorced father of six children when he met Oracene Price in 1979. Oracene already had three daughters of her own—Yetunde, Lyndrea, and Isha. Her first husband had died in 1979. When Oracene became pregnant, she and Richard were married. Their first daughter together, Venus Ebony Starr Williams, was born on June 17, 1980. Richard and Oracene briefly moved their family to Michigan, Oracene's home state. While they lived there, their second daughter, Serena Jameka Williams, was born on September 26, 1981.

Soon after, Richard moved the whole family back to California, to a city south of Los Angeles called Compton.

One day, Richard, who ran a security guard company, got an amazing idea. He was watching a tennis tournament on TV. The winner received a check for a lot of money. Richard decided that his daughters could be tennis champions, too. He dedicated himself to learning all he could about the game and planned to coach his daughters to become superstar players.

He even wrote a book that outlined all that they would have to learn about tennis . . . and how he could teach them.

Richard first tried to get his stepdaughters into tennis, but they didn't take to it like his youngest two daughters did. By the time Venus was four years old, she was hitting hundreds of tennis balls a day. Richard says that she would cry when he said it was time to stop. A year later, Serena joined her sister and took lessons from their father as well.

The courts where they played in Compton were cracked concrete. Weeds and grass often grew up in the cracks, and broken glass littered the corners. The tennis nets were held up with chains and rope.

The fence around the courts was rusty and broken in places. It was a far cry from the perfect courts at tennis or country clubs where many young people learned the game.

The neighborhood around the courts was not much better. Compton was a dangerous place. Many gang members lived there and often caused trouble. Occasionally, the girls heard gunfire near the courts.

"At first," Serena wrote later, "I just thought someone was setting off firecrackers or popping some balloons, but once I learned what the sound meant, it would shake me up pretty good."

Richard collected tennis balls he found near the courts or bought at garage sales. He filled several milk crates with balls and took them to the court for the girls. Sometimes he would roll the crates to the court in a shopping cart. He would do whatever it took to help Venus and Serena become better tennis players. Richard had said that he even lost some teeth fighting to keep the courts safe for the girls!

But as the little girls practiced and practiced, the court slowly became a safer place. Neighbors remember young gang members even standing outside the courts to protect the girls and their dad while they practiced.

Oracene, who worked as a nurse, focused on the girls' home life away from the tennis court. She inspired them to become part of her church, the Jehovah's Witnesses.

All five of Oracene's girls attended meetings at Kingdom Hall on Sundays and sometimes during the week as well. Venus and Serena put in the effort to do what their faith asked of them.

Jehovah's Witnesses

Jehovah's Witnesses follow the Bible's teachings very closely. They refer to God by the name "Jehovah."

Jehovah's Witnesses meet on Sundays and several other days of the week in buildings called Kingdom Halls, not churches. Members invite other people to their gatherings, by going door-to-door and distributing copies of pamphlets and their newspaper, *The Watchtower*.

The faith began in the late 1800s in Pennsylvania. Bible students led by a man named Charles Taze Russell put together the teachings of the Jehovah's Witnesses. They don't vote in elections or celebrate holidays. They believe those things take away from their connection to Jesus.

That included knocking on strangers' doors together, telling people about their faith, and trying to convince them to join their congregation. "People slam doors on us," says Serena, "but that's their problem. We don't take it personally."

Their faith remains a big part of the Williams sisters' lives.

CHAPTER 2
Young Stars

Richard often drove the Williams sisters to the Compton tennis courts in a beat-up old Volkswagen van. He pulled out the middle seat in the van so he could fit the shopping cart filled with tennis balls.

Sometimes the van was so crowded with gear that Serena had to share a seat belt with Venus! Once on the court, the girls hit and hit. Serena remembered that it was always a special thrill when their dad was able to get a can of brand-new tennis balls. New balls bounced better and moved faster than the forgotten ones Richard collected around the edges of the courts.

At home, the two youngest sisters loved their large family, where five sisters shared four beds. Every night, Serena, the youngest, climbed in with one of her sisters. In the evenings, they played a lot of board games. The card game

Uno was a big favorite. Serena was sometimes difficult to play with, though—she hated to lose!

Both parents made sure their daughters worked as hard in school as they did on the tennis court. They attended the local elementary school. Venus was one year ahead of Serena.

Serena followed her big sister Venus in just about everything, even in restaurants. She sometimes just copied whatever Venus ordered.

Lessons with their father continued, and the girls kept getting better and better. By the time Venus was about nine, she started playing against other kids her age in tennis tournaments.

These tournaments were played all around Southern California. Young players were matched by age in events usually played on weekends. Parents and coaches arranged the events, much like youth league baseball or basketball.

From the start, Venus dominated the tournaments. Tall and skinny, she had more power than most kids. Her serve rocketed past her opponents. By the time she finished with junior tennis at the age of eleven, she had won sixty-three matches and lost none.

Serena started a bit later than Venus, but she didn't want to wait to get into tournaments. At an event in 1989, she filled out forms to enter without telling her dad. He found out as he watched her win her first match! Then, Richard sat on the sidelines and watched as the girls played against each other for the first time—in the tournament final! Venus was nine and

Serena was eight. Big sister Venus won, but she gave the trophy to Serena!

Eventually, Serena was allowed to play in more tournaments, one age level below Venus. She performed nearly as well at the junior level, with a record of forty-six wins and three losses.

As the sisters won match after match, the Southern California tennis community took notice. They couldn't help it. Venus and Serena were just about the only Black girls playing. They did not come from a fancy tennis club. Their clothes did not have designer labels. And even the way they played was different. Most young players try to simply hit the ball to a spot where their opponent can't hit it. Venus and Serena used power instead. They slammed the ball hard. They didn't want their opponents to even *see* the ball!

The Williams sisters' success began to get attention outside of California. In 1990, the *New York Times* wrote an article about Venus's success. In 1991, when Venus was still just ten, *Sports Illustrated* did an interview with both sisters. Venus told *Sports Illustrated* that if she did not end up being a tennis player, she wanted to be an astronaut or an archaeologist. Serena said her second career choice would be to become a gymnast or a veterinarian.

Zina Garrison

Because of their growing fame, Venus and Serena were invited to many tennis events where they were able to meet tennis superstars like Chris Evert and Zina Garrison. They were especially happy to meet Garrison, one of the very few African Americans in the sport. They attended a clinic run by tennis legend Billie Jean King. The girls even met former president Ronald Reagan and his wife, Nancy, at a tournament in Palm Springs. Though they were not yet out of elementary school, the Williams sisters were very big news!

As the sisters rose in the ranks, Richard and Oracene worked hard to make sure the girls did not forget the other parts of their lives. If Venus's or Serena's grades slipped, they had to stop playing until their grades improved.

"Too many Black athletes think sports is the only way out," Richard said. "But sports is a vehicle to get an education. I'm looking for my kids to be well balanced."

And tennis was not the sisters' only sport. Venus ran in track events for her elementary school. At one point, she won nineteen races in a row! Her time in the mile when she was only eight years old was 5 minutes, 29 seconds, a time many high school students would be happy with. Serena was good at gymnastics and loved turning cartwheels.

On the court, Venus was tall and strong and had a powerful serve. Serena, too, served the ball very hard. Richard actually thought that someday Serena might become even better than Venus.

Whichever sister came out on top, Richard knew that the road to the top would be hard. But he believed fiercely that he was watching young women who would become the best in the world.

The girls didn't worry about all that. They just wanted to play. At the time, they were each in different levels of youth tennis. They did not play each other in matches, only in practice. That would soon change.

CHAPTER 3
Off to Florida

Richard continued to teach Venus and Serena everything he knew about tennis. Soon, though, he realized that his daughters needed more coaching than he could give them. It was time to hire a professional. Richard called Rick Macci, a coach in Florida who had worked with other young champions, including Jennifer Capriati. In 1990, Capriati, age fourteen, had become the youngest player ever to reach the top ten in the world rankings.

After hearing from

Rick Macci

Richard, Macci flew to Compton. Richard told the coach he would take him and the girls to the "Compton Hills Country Club." But what he meant was the same old beat-up courts they always used. It was a surprise to Macci, who was used to watching young players on fancy, weed-free courts. Seeing the girls play was an even bigger surprise. He was impressed by how well they played. Not only were they strong for their age, they were also fast and graceful. But he also saw that the girls would need better coaching to improve their game.

One thing he did not have to coach them about: their desire to win.

"Venus and Serena had a deep down burning desire to fight and compete at this age," he would later write. "I believed that both Venus and Serena had champion written all over them."

Macci believed that he could make them even better than they already were. But to do so, they would have to leave their California home and move to Florida. That's where Macci's tennis academy was located.

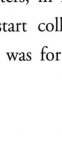

In 1991, the Williams family packed up an RV and drove across the country. The move was hard on some of the older sisters; in fact, Yetunde stayed in California to start college. But Richard and Oracene knew it was for the best.

Once in Florida, where they moved into a rented house, the girls practiced "six hours a day, six days a week for four years," said Macci. The girls hit hundreds of serves every day.

The sisters also took lessons at a private school that was part of the tennis academy. It was tennis and school, tennis and school, every day.

Richard believed that practice and coaching,

and not more competition, would make the girls better. So Venus and Serena took more than three years off from playing in tournaments. They spent that time studying and practicing tennis while nearly all other players their age were in dozens of tournaments a year. Would their lack of game experience prevent the girls from succeeding?

By the time Venus was fourteen, it was time to change that routine. She believed she was ready to turn pro—to begin playing tennis at a professional level. She wanted to start playing against the best players in the world. Some young teenagers, like Tracy Austin and Jennifer Capriati, had already become champions.

Then in 1994, the Women's Tennis Association (WTA) passed a new rule saying that no one could turn pro before she was fifteen. The rule did not apply to Venus, however. She was allowed to join the WTA because she had already signed up before the rule was passed.

Venus played her first pro tournament in October 1994. She lost in one of the early rounds. But she was only fourteen, after all.

All the attention Venus had received in her young life—magazine articles, TV interviews, and her professional debut at a young age—paid off quickly. Before she had won a single tournament, she signed a contract with international sports and fitness company Reebok that paid her $12 million over five years. Her unique story and potential for success made Reebok eager to see her play wearing their brand of clothes and tennis shoes. It was a shocking deal for someone so young.

The Women's Tennis Association

Women have played in professional tennis tournaments for many decades, but it wasn't until 1970 that the Women's Tennis Association (WTA) was founded by top pro player Billie Jean King and others.

In its first full year, 1971, the WTA organized nineteen tournaments for prize money totaling more than $300,000.

The WTA has grown into the largest sports organization for women in the world. Each year it hosts more than fifty international tournaments. The total prize money now tops more than $130 million annually. The WTA publishes the official weekly rankings of players. They also establish rules for who is eligible to play in the WTA.

Right after she turned fifteen, Serena joined the WTA and played in her first pro tournament. The German shoe and sportswear company Puma offered her a huge contract in 1998. Richard's plan to turn Venus and Serena into champions was not yet complete, but his daughters had certainly turned around the family's fortunes.

The Williams family bought a large mansion in Palm Beach, Florida. The estate had two full tennis courts without a crack in them.

The girls left Macci's academy and Richard took over coaching them himself again. They hired private tutors to help them with schoolwork.

On the path leading from the house to the family courts, Richard put up signs. The sisters read them as they walked toward the courts each day. One read, VENUS YOU MUST TAKE CONTROL OF YOUR FUTURE. Another, directed at Serena, said, YOU MUST LEARN TO USE MORE TOP SPIN ON THE BALL.

How did such young girls, just barely teenagers, have the drive to work so hard? Certainly Richard's coaching and encouragement played a big part. But the Williams sisters have always said that they were the ones who pushed their careers forward. Richard pointed to the road, but the hardworking and talented sisters did the difficult work on the court.

The Williams sisters were ready to take the professional tennis world by storm.

CHAPTER 4
A Rivalry Grows

Though they were pros, the Williams sisters played in very few tournaments in 1995 and 1996. They continued to live and practice and do schoolwork in Florida. Richard continued to encourage the girls and help them to develop their powerful serves. At a time when most players' serves reached only about 100 miles per hour, Venus could sometimes hit the ball 120 miles per hour! The sisters moved faster than other tennis players and could get to shots many pros could not reach. They were improving day by day and were noticed for beating higher-ranked players.

They were also getting attention for how they looked and dressed. Most female tennis players wore plain pastel or white clothes.

The Williams sisters had a more colorful sense of style. Oracene braided her daughters' hair, and added bright beads to the braids. When playing in England at Wimbledon, for example, Venus wore purple and dark green beads in her hair—

the colors of the tournament. The sisters also wore tennis skirts and dresses in bright colors.

Fans and reporters took notice, and not always in a positive way. Some tennis experts and journalists felt that such colorful gear was out of place in the world of professional tennis.

Later in her career, Serena commented on her style, saying, "I just think I represent all females out there who believe in themselves. It doesn't matter what you look like, it's all about having confidence in *you*."

Some people did not like how the girls showed emotion when they made a great play or won a big game. For the most part, women in pro tennis did not celebrate or shout after winning a point or a match.

In fact, the rules still prohibit the players from talking to or yelling at their opponents while the ball is in play. Tennis fans are also expected to be very quiet as each point begins. However, after winning tough points or big games, the Williams sisters, often shouted encouragement at themselves or let out a big whoop.

Venus spoke out about her new place in the game during a 1997 interview. "I'm tall, I'm black, everything's different about me . . . face the facts."

By late 1997, Venus was getting attention for more than her style. At top tournaments, the best players (usually about sixteen or thirty-two, depending on the size of the event) are given a "seeding"—a rank against the other players. The rest of the players are not given a seed and have to play tougher matches. At the 1997 US Open, in the newly named Arthur Ashe Stadium in Queens, New York, seventeen-year-old Venus did not receive one of the seeds.

She still battled through many top players to make the final. She was the first unseeded player since 1958 to do so. Though she lost that final to Martina Hingis, it was a huge moment for the Williams family. But it was soon overshadowed.

In interviews with reporters, Richard, who was not at the tournament, said that people were against Venus, her style, and her attitude because she was Black. Venus responded that she just wanted to talk about tennis. "I think this moment in the first year in Arthur Ashe Stadium, it all represents everyone being together, everyone having a chance to play," she said. "So I think this is definitely ruining the mood, these questions about racism."

As the sisters continued to move up the ranks in the world of professional tennis, their race continued to be part of their story. They mostly ignored the questions from reporters or the comments from people in the stands and charged ahead, being true to themselves and winning again and again.

"Whenever tennis had [asked] them to be like everyone else . . . the sisters have always famously declined," wrote a reporter a few years later. "They are black in a sport where practically no one is black."

While the tennis world buzzed about the sisters, they faced another issue: playing each other. Since they had started back in Compton, they had

Arthur Ashe (1943–1993)

Arthur Ashe grew up in Virginia and later graduated from the University of California–Los Angeles. In 1975, he became the first African American man to be ranked No. 1 in tennis in the world, and he was also the first to win Wimbledon, the US Open, and the Australian Open.

He retired in 1980. In 1988, doctors discovered that he had been infected with HIV/AIDS from blood received during a heart operation. He became a leading activist, working to educate people about the disease. The main stadium at the USTA Tennis Center—where the US Open is played each year—is named Arthur Ashe Stadium in his honor.

rarely faced each other in a match that counted. As juniors, they were in different age divisions. As they began entering pro events together, however, it was sister vs. sister.

At the 1998 Australian Open, Venus beat Serena to knock her out of the tournament.

"It wasn't fun eliminating my little sister," Venus said, "but I have to be tough. . . . Since I'm older, I have the feeling I should win."

When they weren't playing each other, they celebrated together. In early 1998, Venus won her first pro tournament in Oklahoma City. The next year, the two sisters became the first sisters to each win a tournament on the same day! Venus won again in Oklahoma while Serena won in Paris.

Venus and Serena also excelled at doubles tennis. In doubles, teams of two players face off against each other. Paired with Justin Gimelstob in mixed doubles (one male and one female player), Venus won the 1998 Australian and French Open doubles championships.

Teaming with Max Mirnyi, Serena took home titles at Wimbledon and the US Open. That gave the sisters all four Grand Slam mixed doubles titles in one year, an all-time professional tennis first.

What Are the Grand Slams?

There are four tennis tournaments that are considered to be the most important professional tennis events in the world. Together, they are known as the Grand Slam. (Each individual event is called a Grand Slam, too.) The tournaments are played on three different surfaces to challenge the players' skills.

The Grand Slams are:

- Australian Open: Played early in the year on hard courts in Melbourne, Australia.

- French Open: Played in Paris on red-clay courts.

- Wimbledon: Played on grass courts in Wimbledon, England, officially called "The Championships."

- United States Open: Played on hard courts in New York City.

A player has to win *all four* of these events in the same year to win the Grand Slam. The last woman to do this was Steffi Graf in 1988. The last man was Rod Laver in 1969.

The Williams sisters also played together as doubles partners. They used their family advantage to win their first two pro doubles events in 1998.

Through all of their early success, they were both still teenagers. To have some fun as they  traveled from tournament to tournament, Venus came up with the idea for a newsletter. The girls worked together to write, edit, design, and print their *Tennis Monthly Recap*. They interviewed other players and included notes on things they saw and heard at pro matches. When each issue was ready, they distributed it to other professional players.

In 1998, Venus finished her lessons and graduated from the Driftwood Academy, a private high school. Serena graduated the following year. In the years to come, both girls took college classes online, studying languages, history, business, and fashion.

That year also saw the teens' first matchup in a professional tournament final, the Lipton Championships in Florida. Venus won that match, but Serena had her moment soon after.

At the 1999 US Open, Serena became the first African American woman to win the event since Althea Gibson in 1958.

President Bill Clinton called Serena right after the US Open to congratulate her. "It was very exciting," Serena said. "I thought for sure my day couldn't get any better. Next thing I knew, someone was telling me, 'the president of the United States wants to talk.'"

Up to this point, Venus had been the bigger star. By winning the first Grand Slam singles title in the Williams family, Serena positioned herself to move past her older sister.

Althea Gibson (1927–2003)

Growing up in New York City, Althea Gibson was a great athlete. But she had to overcome the racism of professional sports to take her place among tennis's greatest stars.

Gibson was the girls' champion of the American Tennis Association (ATA) in 1944 and 1945, and the women's champion from 1947 to 1956. The ATA was for African Americans only. The United States Lawn Tennis Association did not allow Black players in its tournaments.

In 1950, Gibson changed that when she became the first Black player ever to play in the US National Championships, the top tournament in America (later called the US Open). The next year, she was the first Black player at Wimbledon, too.

In 1956, she won the French Open. In both 1957 and 1958 she won the US Open *and* Wimbledon.

Althea Gibson was voted into the International Tennis Hall of Fame in 1971.

CHAPTER 5
Tennis Ups and Downs

The Williams sisters' rivalry continued in 2000. At Wimbledon, the Grand Slam event in England, they faced each other in the semifinals. Venus won that match and went on to win the tournament, becoming the first African American to be Wimbledon champion since Arthur Ashe in 1975. Venus and Serena combined to win the women's double title as well.

The sisters represented the United States in doubles at the 2000 Summer Olympic Games in Sydney, Australia, in September. Venus and Serena defeated a team from the Netherlands in the final and won the gold medal. Venus also competed in singles and won another gold medal!

Back on tour, the sisters combined to win the doubles title at the 2001 Australian Open.

That meant the pair had completed a career Grand Slam in doubles. They were the first sisters ever to do that.

As the Williams sisters won match after match, it seemed like people were paying less and less attention to the color of their skin, and just admiring their tennis skills and their celebrity status.

In 2001, however, a sad event brought up racial issues once again. At a tournament in Indian Wells, California, Venus suffered a knee injury and heat exhaustion. She told tournament doctors that she would not be able to play her match against Serena. Many people had come to see the sisters play, but they were not told by officials that Venus could not play until about five minutes before the match. The fans became very upset and booed loudly. Some accused Venus of faking her injury so that Serena would make the final. But Venus really was injured.

The next day was much worse. As Serena walked onto the court for the final match, the fans, still angry, began booing again. Soon, it was more than boos. People called her terrible names and some shouted, "Go back to Compton!" Richard got angry at the fans, and that made them boo and shout even more.

Throughout the match, the fans rooted against Serena because they were mad at Venus for pulling out of the earlier match. Serena later wrote in her autobiography, "All I could see was a sea of rich people—mostly older, mostly white . . . standing and booing . . . It's tough to ignore fourteen thousand screaming people—especially when they're screaming at you."

It was shocking. But Serena somehow fought through the noise and anger and won the match and the tournament. She was crying as she left the court.

"As a family we were all hurt," said her older sister Isha. "It stayed with us a long time."

In fact, the Williams sisters said they would never play in the Indian Wells tournament again, even though it might hurt their careers to avoid it.

The news was good in other places, however. Later that year, the sisters met in the final match of the 2001 US Open. They were the first sisters to accomplish that in a Grand Slam event since 1884! The match was shown on prime-time television—a first for a Grand Slam women's tennis final—and 22.7 million people watched as Venus beat Serena.

CHAPTER 6
A Powerful Pair

In the early part of their careers, Venus had been the more successful of the two Williams sisters. She had beaten Serena in most matches they played and she was ranked higher. In fact, on February 25, 2002, she reached the No. 1 spot in the world rankings. But as that year went on, Serena overtook her older sister.

She won her first French Open, defeating Venus in the final. Venus stayed for the trophy ceremony and took pictures of her sister with the award. By May, Serena had moved up behind Venus to No. 2 in the rankings, another all-time first for sisters. Serena then beat Venus at Wimbledon and the US Open. In early 2003, she made it four in a row over her sister by winning the Australian Open. Her four straight Grand Slam wins created the first "Serena Slam."

It was not a complete Grand Slam because her wins came in two different years, but it was a huge accomplishment.

Venus's and Serena's tremendous success in the world of professional tennis was only a part of what the sisters had set out to accomplish. They each had personal interests they wanted to explore off the tennis courts. And in the early 2000s, they both started new businesses.

Venus—who loved art and design—became a licensed interior decorator and formed her own company called V*Starr. When she wasn't practicing tennis, she would often work in the V*Starr office. She helped find clients, make plans for new business, and create interior designs for homes and offices.

How Do Rankings Work?

The women's rankings are created each week by the WTA. (The Association of Tennis Professionals calculates the rankings for the men.) The WTA list is based on points earned in the previous fifty-two weeks. So just winning one big event does not make a player No. 1. She has to build up a series of high finishes until she has enough points to reach the top.

From 1987 to 1991, Steffi Graf set a record by remaining at No. 1 for 186 straight weeks. In 2016, Serena Williams tied that record.

Serena became the head of
her own fashion line, called
Aneres (her name spelled
backward). She designed
clothes that were sold
in stores and online.
And she wore her own
brand. Aneres got even more
attention when a Miss
America contestant wore
one of Serena's dresses
in 2004. Later, Serena's
clothes would be sold on
the Home Shopping Network,
under her full name—spelled forward this time!

Their sponsors, Reebok and Puma, continued
to be part of the sisters' business plans, but other
brands, like Doublemint gum, McDonald's, and
several clothing companies hired them, too. By
this time, the Williams sisters were making much

more money off the court than they were making on it.

The sisters were in demand for their winning personalities and strong sense of style as much as for their professional success. They appeared on magazine covers and were interviewed on talk shows. They posed for fashion shoots. They had become role models for many young girls—of all colors.

The popular Williams sisters were on top of the tennis world. The next couple of years, however, would be far from happy.

CHAPTER 7
Overcoming Tragedy

By 2003, the sisters were very busy following their dreams. Venus lived in a house in Florida the sisters had built together. Serena spent most of her time at a condominium in Los Angeles. Their parents had separated a year earlier. Richard spent time in California, while Oracene usually stayed with one of the sisters in Florida.

Their older sister Yetunde Price, meanwhile, had remained in southern California.

Yetunde Price

She lived in a large home in a quiet suburb. And she sometimes visited their old friends in Compton. On September 14, 2003, Yetunde was riding in a car in Compton when shots were fired at the car. Yetunde was hit by a bullet. She died of her injuries.

The entire Williams family was shocked by this sudden death. Serena was in Toronto filming a TV show, along with her sister Lyndrea. They rushed home. Venus was in Florida. Everyone returned to Compton for Yetunde's funeral. "It was awful, just awful," Serena wrote later. But the family stuck together as it always had. "We held on to each other for dear life," Serena wrote.

The following few years were very hard for the Williams sisters. Sad about the loss of their sister, they also had to deal with injuries: Muscles in Venus's stomach and Serena's left knee both required medical attention. Serena also began treatment for depression. In 2006, her ranking fell all the way to 139. Neither of the sisters won as many matches as they had in the past.

Venus dropped back to a No. 9 world ranking, partly because she had played fewer matches in 2004 and 2005. At the 2005 Wimbledon tournament, she was seeded No. 14, her worst

seeding in a long time. However, she rallied to win her fifth Grand Slam title. No player with a seed number that high had ever won Wimbledon!

Serena found another way to rally back to the top of her game. Before she headed south for the 2007 Australian Open, she traveled to Africa for the first time. In Ghana and Senegal, she met with young people, gave tennis lessons, and brought medicine and food to poor villages.

She even helped distribute bed nets to keep dangerous disease-carrying mosquitoes away from villagers. After meeting with Senegal's president, she decided to help build a school there. She also toured some of the sites on the coast from which African slaves were taken to North America.

"Somehow, that first trip to Africa lifted me from my doldrums and set me back down on a positive path," she later wrote.

CHAPTER 8
Ups and Downs . . . and Ups

Re-inspired by her trip to Africa, Serena arrived at the 2007 Australian Open. She had not played very much after Yetunde's death and her long trip. While some tennis experts thought she had no chance, she had a surprise for them. Though she was not even given one of the seedings, she stormed past opponent after opponent. Serena ended up winning her third Australian Open!

After the final, she said, "Most of all I would like to dedicate this win to my sister who's not here. Her name is Yetunde, and I just love her so much."

In 2007, Venus used her influence to improve earnings for women's tennis professionals. Up to that point, men were paid more money for winning Grand Slam tournaments than women. Venus did not think this was fair. She wrote an article in the *Times* of London that said: "The message I like to convey to women and girls across the globe is that there is no glass ceiling [which means a barrier to success]. My fear is that Wimbledon is loudly and clearly sending the opposite message."

Thanks to Venus, Wimbledon changed its rules and now women and men earn the same amount for their wins.

In 2008, Venus earned the newly increased prize money by winning Wimbledon again, beating Serena in a Grand Slam final for the first time since the 2001 US Open. Then Venus and Serena completed their comeback with another gold medal in doubles at the 2008 Summer Olympics in Beijing, China.

By 2009, Serena was earning more than any other WTA player. But later that year, in a tough match at the 2009 US Open, Serena got mad at the officials. She thought they had made a bad call against her and she shouted at them. This is against the rules of professional tennis.

Because of Serena's outburst, the officials awarded a point to her opponent. Upset and frustrated, Serena lost the match. She was later fined $82,500 and was warned she could face more penalties if she did it again.

However, she continued to be the player to beat in the years that followed.

Venus had reached No. 1 again briefly in 2010, but then injured her knee. She was unable to play for several months. Soon after she returned, she was diagnosed with Sjögren's syndrome. This rare disease was treated with medication, but the disease often made her weak. In about a year, her ranking had fallen all the way to 105.

As Venus stopped playing to deal with her illness, Serena was hit by her own health crisis. First, in July 2010, she accidentally stepped on a piece of broken glass. The cut on her foot, which required twelve stitches, kept her off the court for many weeks. While she was recovering, blood clots were found in her lungs.

She needed an operation right away. It was a very dangerous illness.

"I just thought she was going to die," her father said.

Some people thought that Serena would stop playing tennis for good. Those people did not know just how tough Serena really was.

A year later, she had recovered enough to play in the 2012 Summer Olympics in London. She won the singles gold medal. Venus battled back from her own illness to join Serena in London. Together, they won their third gold medal in doubles.

The sisters had faced some tough challenges, but they faced them the same way they did all their tennis opponents—with courage.

CHAPTER 9
Sports Sisters of the Year

At the beginning of 2015, Serena—now age thirty-three—was older than most of the other professional women players, but she was still ranked No. 1. She began the year by winning the Australian Open.

In Australia, Serena showed just how much she had matured. In an early match, she lost a point for yelling as her opponent hit the ball. Would she be in trouble again? This time, she knew how to handle things.

"I just kind of laughed [it off]," Serena said. "A few years ago I wouldn't have been able to laugh. I haven't lost that part of me; I'm very passionate on the court, but I've learned to be fierce more on the inside."

Following her Australian win, Serena surprised everyone and decided to return to Indian Wells and the tournament where she and Venus had been treated so badly.

"I was brought up to forgive people," Serena said, "and I felt that I wasn't doing what I was taught."

She returned to the same court where she had been booed in 2001. This time, she was greeted with cheers and applause that brought her and her family to tears. Serena used the event to call attention to the ongoing problems of racism in America.

"It's a great opportunity," Serena said. "If you're in a position where you can stand up and be a role model, then why not do it? I feel this is a perfect opportunity and a perfect [place] for me to do it. I'm looking forward to letting the whole world know, if it's something that wasn't right, hurt you, hurt your family, you can just come out and be strong and say, 'I'm still going to be here. I'm going to survive. I'm going to be the best person I can be.'"

Though she had to come out of the tournament early after suffering a knee injury, this time she was cheered as she left the court. Later she said, "Everyone always asked, 'What was your greatest moment in tennis?' and I always said it hasn't happened. But I think it has happened now, and that was going back to Indian Wells and playing."

At the next Grand Slam event that year, the French Open, she showed just how strong a competitor she was. Late in the tournament, Serena got the flu and had a very high fever. But she overcame it to win the final.

"It took her a week to get okay. It was a victorious moment, but it was scary," said Isha, who was at the event with her sister. Serena thanked the fans in Paris with a speech she made in French!

At Wimbledon in July, she wrapped up her second Serena Slam, winning all four Grand Slams in a row. It was not an "official" Grand Slam annual championship, since she did not win all four in the same year. At thirty-three, she was also the oldest woman in more than a hundred years to win *any* Grand Slam singles tournament. Now attention turned to whether she could win all four Grand Slams in a single year—a feat not accomplished since Steffi Graf did it in 1988.

At the US Open, the attention of the world was on her. Millions tuned in to see what they hoped would be the biggest sports story of the year. Instead, Serena suffered one of the biggest upsets in tennis history, losing in the semifinal to 43rd-ranked Roberta Vinci. Serena was disappointed, but knew that she would once again bounce back.

Even with the loss, Serena was named by *Sports Illustrated* as the magazine's Sportsperson

of the Year. It was a great honor, and she became the first solo Black woman to have that distinction.

In 2016, Serena was still number one. Venus continued to be in the top ten.

Venus was also making news for the success

of her clothing line. Called EleVen, the company made fitness and tennis clothes for women. Venus worked on all the designs and also did some of the modeling. She wore EleVen clothes while playing at Wimbledon that year.

Both women continued to play at the highest levels.

At the 2017 Australian Open, the sisters again faced off in a Grand Slam final. At thirty-six, Venus was the oldest woman ever to play in an Australian final. Serena won the match and set a new record with twenty-three Grand Slam championsips. They never forget that they are family. "It's nice to be able to spend time together," said Venus. "I've always been a big sister. It's the best job in the world. I think probably [Serena] thinks being a little sister is the best job in the world."

In 2022, Serena decided to step away from professional competition. Beyond tennis, Serena had gotten married and become a mother.

She was excited to spend less time on the court and more time with her new family.

The sisters continue to be proud African American role models.

"A lot of people come up to me and don't ask for my autograph, they just say thanks," Serena once said. Later she added, "I think it really helps people believe that, you know what, if they did it, I can, too. I feel honored that I was chosen to have an opportunity to be that role model for those people in the inner city and the inner communities."

One of the more lasting influences of Venus and Serena Williams can be found on tennis courts around the country. The United States Tennis Association (USTA) reports that many more African American and Hispanic children have started playing the game since the Williams sisters became famous. Katrina Adams, the first Black female to be president of the USTA, calls the sisters "our greatest ambassadors."

After winning her seventh Wimbledon title in 2016, Serena said, "Anyone, any kid out there that wants to be something, has dreams. I've had great dreams . . . and I did have hope. That's all you really need."

Few athletes have had the worldwide impact on their sport that Venus and Serena have had on women's tennis. They have dominated the sport with their discipline and drive. The world of professional tennis will never be the same because of the amazing Williams sisters!

Timeline of Venus and Serena Williams's Lives

1980	Venus is born in California
1981	Serena is born in Michigan
1984	Venus starts playing tennis, coached by her father, Richard. Serena starts soon after
1991	The Williams family moves to Florida to work with coach Rick Macci
1997	Venus becomes the first unseeded player since 1958 to reach finals of US Open
1999	Serena is the first of the sisters to win a Grand Slam
2000	Venus wins her first Grand Slam event at Wimbledon
	The sisters team up to win an Olympic gold medal in doubles
2002	Venus reaches the No. 1 ranking for the first time; Serena does the same later in the year
2003	Serena wins the Australian Open to complete the "Serena Slam" for the first time
2007	Venus wins Wimbledon again
2008	The sisters win another Olympic doubles gold medal
2010	Serena is No. 1 and Venus is No. 2 in the rankings in June
2012	Serena wins her first Olympic singles gold medal
	Serena is named *Sports Illustrated* Sportsperson of the Year
2016	Serena wins the Australian Open and sets a new twenty-three Grand Slam record

Timeline of the World

1980	Mount Saint Helens volcano erupts in Washington State
1981	Sandra Day O'Connor is the first woman named to the US Supreme Court
1986	The space shuttle *Challenger* explodes shortly after takeoff
1990	Nelson Mandela is freed from jail in South Africa; he would become its president in 1994
1991	The Soviet Union collapses, breaking up into Russia and many new independent countries
	The World Wide Web is available for the first time
1994	The Channel Tunnel, connecting England and France, opens for business
2001	On September 11, terrorists attack the United States, killing more than 3,000 people
2006	International astronomers change Pluto from a planet to a dwarf planet
2007	Apple sells the first iPhone
2008	Barack Obama is elected the first African American president of the United States
2011	A terrible earthquake causes a tsunami that ravages the east coast of Japan
2012	*Voyager 1* becomes the first human-made object to leave the solar system
2015	Queen Elizabeth II becomes the longest-serving monarch ever in Great Britain

Bibliography

* Books for young readers

* Buckley, James Jr. *Venus and Serena Williams*. Milwaukee: World Almanac Library, 2003.

Macci, Rick, with Jim Martz. *Macci Magic: Extracting Greatness from Yourself and Others*. New York: New Chapter Media, 2013.

Price, S.L. "Serena Williams Is *Sports Illustrated's* Sportsperson of the Year." *Sports Illustrated*, December 21, 2015.

Williams, Serena, with Daniel Paisner. *On the Line*. New York: Grand Central Publishing, 2009.

* Williams, Venus, and Serena Williams, with Hilary Beard. *Venus and Serena: Serving from the Hip: 10 Rules for Living, Loving, and Winning*. Boston: HMH Books for Young Readers, 2005.